POISONOUS CREATURES
INVESTIGATE!
T0021513
Beware the
POISON
DART FROG!
Ursula Pang
Enslow
PUBLISHING

Please visit our website, www.enslow.com. For a free color catalog of all our high-quality books, call toll free 1-800-398-2504 or fax 1-877-980-4454.

Library of Congress Cataloging-in-Publication Data

Names: Pang, Ursula, author.
Title: Beware the poison dart frog! / Ursula Pang.
Description: New York : Enslow Publishing, [2023] | Series: Poisonous creatures | Includes index.
Identifiers: LCCN 2021044927 (print) | LCCN 2021044928 (ebook) | ISBN 9781978527485 (library binding) | ISBN 9781978527461 (paperback) | ISBN 9781978527478 (6 pack) | ISBN 9781978527492 (ebook)
Subjects: LCSH: Dendrobatidae–Juvenile literature. | Poisonous animals–Juvenile literature.
Classification: LCC QL668.E233 P36 2023 (print) | LCC QL668.E233 (ebook) | DDC 597.8/77–dc23
LC record available at https://lccn.loc.gov/2021044927
LC ebook record available at https://lccn.loc.gov/2021044928

Portions of this work were originally authored by Laura L. Sullivan and published as *The Poison Dart Frog*. All new material in this edition was authored by Ursula Pang.

Published in 2023 by
Enslow Publishing
29 E. 21st Street
New York, NY 10010

Designer: Katelyn E. Reynolds
Interior Layout: Tanya Dellaccio
Editor: Greg Roza

Photo credits: Cover Orlata Ievgeniia 24/Shutterstock.com; background texture Vector Tradition/Shutterstock.com; pp. 5 (main), 13 reptiles4all/Shutterstock.com; p. 5 (inset) Charles Bergman/Shutterstock.com; pp. 6, 7, 9 (main), 23 (top), 26 Thorsten Spoerlein/Shutterstock.com; p. 9 (inset) Lucia Christine Bucklin/Shutterstock.com; pp.11 (frog), 17 (inset), 21, 23 (middle), 23 (bottom), 25 Dirk Ercken/Shutterstock.com; p. 11 (map) Raevsky Lab/Shutterstock.com; p.12 Milan Zygmunt/Shutterstock.com; p. 15 Helena1/Shutterstock.com; p. 17 (main) Daniel Karfik; p. 18 Uwe Bergwitz/Shutterstock.com; p. 19 SL-Photography/Shutterstock.com; p. 20 Alex Stemmers/Shutterstock.com; p. 24 Ghiglione Claudio/Shutterstock.com; p. 27 Marcin Kadziolka/Shutterstock.com; p. 29 Gorodenkoff/Shutterstock.com.

Printed in the United States of America

CPSIA compliance information: Batch #CSENS23: For further information contact Enslow Publishing, New York, New York, at 1-800-398-2504.

CONTENTS

WORDS IN THE GLOSSARY APPEAR IN **BOLD** TYPE THE FIRST TIME THEY ARE USED IN THE TEXT.

RAIN FOREST DWELLERS

You can find poison dart frogs in parts of Central America and South America. They're a group of brightly colored and highly poisonous amphibians. Amphibians are **cold-blooded** vertebrates, which means they have a backbone. They have smooth skin and spend part of their life in the water and part on land.

There are more than 170 kinds of poison dart frogs. Some of them are only mildly toxic. A few aren't toxic at all. Others, though, have enough poison in their bodies to kill any animal or person that tries to eat or harm them.

POISON DART FROGS ARE DIURNAL. THIS MEANS THEY'RE ACTIVE DURING THE DAY. MOST RAIN FOREST FROGS ARE ACTIVE AT NIGHT.

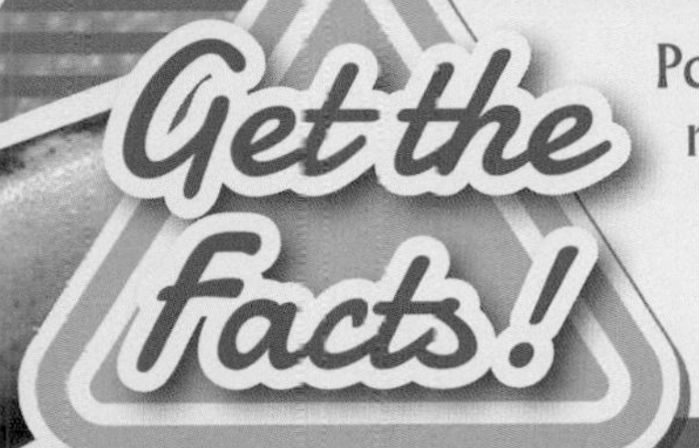

Poison dart frogs live in hot, wet places like rain forests. This is their habitat. Rain forests are being destroyed for land and wood. This has caused some poison dart frogs to move closer to farms and houses.

FROG EGGS

Mating begins with a dance. The male and female frogs stroke each other's skin. They look for good spots for the female to lay her eggs.

Eggs must be **fertilized** before a tadpole can grow in an egg. Poison dart

Get the Facts!

Male poison dart frogs use a loud "croak" to call out to female frogs. A forest full of these frogs can make a lot of noise! They also use loud sounds to claim territory and when they are in pain.

POISON DART FROGS OFTEN LAY THEIR EGGS IN MOIST PILES OF LEAVES ON THE GROUND. SOME MAY LAY EGGS ON THE LARGE LEAVES OF LIVING PLANTS.

frog eggs are fertilized outside the body. The female lays between one and forty eggs in a moist place. The male then fertilizes them. It is common for both the mother and father to stay with the eggs. Poison dart frogs usually take care of their young.

CARING FOR TADPOLES

Male poison dart frogs often watch the eggs before they **hatch**. Tadpoles hatch after about two weeks. The mother or both parents will carry them on their backs to water. They often choose a plant called a bromeliad. This plant grows high in tree branches. It forms a cup at its base to store water. Both parents may take care of their babies until the tadpoles mature.

The tadpoles eat the small creatures that live in the bromeliad water. The mother will lay unfertilized eggs for the tadpoles to eat too.

POISON DART FROGS USUALLY LIVE BETWEEN THREE AND TEN YEARS. WHEN KEPT AS PETS, SOME SPECIES CAN LIVE UP TO TWENTY YEARS.

Most kinds of poison dart frog have tadpoles that will eat nearly everything they can. This includes algae and bugs.

BROMELIAD

GETTING TO KNOW THE POISON DART FROG

Scientific Name

All poison dart frogs are in the family *Dendrobatidae*. That word means "tree climber."

Species

Because poison dart frogs often have different color patterns within the same **species**, scientists are still classifying some of them. There are approximately 170 species. These include the golden poison dart frog, the strawberry poison dart frog, and the blue poison dart frog.

Range

Poison dart frogs live in parts of Central and South America. They live in Costa Rica, Panama, Brazil, Colombia, Ecuador, Peru, Bolivia, Nicaragua, Venezuela, Suriname, Guyana, and French Guiana.

Size

The smallest poison dart frogs are less than 1 inch (2.5 cm) long. The largest reach about 2.4 inches (6 cm) long. They usually weigh less than 1 ounce (28.35 g).

Fun Fact

Some frogs that aren't poisonous **mimic** the bright colors of poison dart frogs. Predators don't eat them because they think they are poisonous too.

CENTRAL AMERICA

THIS MAP SHOWS IN GREEN WHERE POISON DART FROGS LIVE IN THE WILD.

SOUTH AMERICA

TOXIC!

Poison dart frogs have toxins, or poisons, in their skin. These poisons cause harm if the frogs are eaten or if the poison gets in a cut on the skin. Some poison dart frogs are among the most poisonous creatures on Earth. The golden poison dart frog has enough poison to kill 10 to 20 adult people. It also can kill two adult African elephants, or 20,000 mice!

THE DEATHSTALKER SCORPION, SHOWN HERE, USES ITS STINGER TO **INJECT** DEADLY VENOM INTO OTHER CREATURES.

Poison dart frogs **secrete** poison from their skin. When they sense danger, the frogs make a milky poison from glands on their neck and back.

Get the Facts!

A toxin is something harmful made by a plant or animal. A toxin is called a poison if it causes harm when eaten, breathed in, or **absorbed** through the skin. A toxin is called a venom when it's injected with fangs or stingers.

NEUROTOXINS

Scientists think poison dart frogs make toxins from the food they eat. They mostly eat ants, mites, centipedes, and small beetles. They take the chemicals they need from these animals to make their poison. Each species makes a different toxin based on their diet.

Poison dart frogs make neurotoxins. These can block the signals being sent from one nerve to another. The nerves then cannot signal muscles to move. The lungs will not be able to take in oxygen. Also, the heart will not be able to beat. A person would probably die about 10 minutes after swallowing poison dart frog neurotoxins.

THERE IS NO GOOD TREATMENT FOR POISON DART FROG POISONING. LUCKILY, HUMAN DEATHS FROM POISON DART FROGS ARE VERY RARE. NOT MANY PEOPLE TRY TO EAT A POISON DART FROG.

Poison dart frogs that are born in a zoo or as a pet eat different food. This food doesn't have the matter in it needed to make poison. Pet poison dart frogs are safe to touch.

TOO PRETTY TO EAT

Most frogs want to blend in with their surroundings to hide from predators. Poison dart frogs, however, changed over time to show off beautiful colors. Poison dart frogs want everyone to see them! When a predator sees those bright colors, it knows to stay away.

Other frogs have evolved so they look like colorful poison dart frogs. Predators think they are toxic too. A few species of poison dart frogs don't make poison. These kinds have duller brown skin to help them blend in with their surroundings. Without poison, they have to hide.

POISON DART FROGS DEVELOPED THEIR COLORS TO WARN PREDATORS AGAINST EATING THEM.

Even tadpoles and baby frogs can make poison. The unfertilized eggs the mother feeds them have the matter in them that make the poison.

NAME GAME

Why are these kinds of frogs called poison dart frogs? The danger of poison dart frogs has long been known to the **indigenous** people of Central and South America. Some indigenous groups coat the tips of their hunting darts in the frog's poison.

Poison dart frogs use their poison to stay safe from predators. They don't use it to hunt. Indigenous people, however, use the poison strictly for hunting.

THIS MAN IS USING A BLOWGUN TO SHOOT A POISON DART AT AN ANIMAL IN THE TREES.

Carefully, hunters trap the frogs and scare them until they secrete poison. They then rub their blowgun darts in the poison. Whatever they hit with the poisoned dart will die. The poison remains effective for a year or more, even after it has dried.

POISON HUNTERS

The indigenous groups that commonly use poison dart frogs include the Emberá, Noanamá, and Cuna groups from Colombia. They've developed techniques to catch, keep, and use the frogs to poison their dart tips for hunting.

The Emberá tribes keep baskets of golden poison dart frogs, which they call *kokoe*. When they need to coat a dart, they carefully hold the frog down with a stick and rub the dart tip over the frog's back. The frog is not harmed and is released after coating a few darts.

GOLDEN POISON DART FROGS HAVE BUMPS AROUND THEIR MOUTH THAT SOMETIMES LOOK LIKE TEETH.

The Emberá is Colombia's third-largest indigenous group. Smaller groups of Emberá live in Panama and Equador. The Emberá are sometimes called the Chocó, which is what the first Spanish settlers called them.

THE MOST DANGEROUS

Scientists have discovered that the brighter a poison dart frog's colors, the more poisonous it likely is. The deadliest frogs are from the genus Phyllobates, especially the species *Phyllobates terribilis, Phyllobates bicolor,* and *Phyllobates aurotaenia.*

These three species secrete a neurotoxin called batrachotoxin, which is one of the deadliest toxins on Earth! Indigenous groups have long known how deadly these species are, and have used their poison to coat hunting darts and arrows for many years.

Phyllobates terribilis

Common name: golden poison frog

Phyllobates bicolor

Common names: black- legged poison frog, green-legged poison frog, bicolored poison frog

Phyllobates aurotaenia

Common name: Kokoe poison frog

AMPHIBIAN ILLNESS

A huge threat to poison dart frogs is a disease called chytrid fungus. This disease kills many species of frogs, toads, salamanders, and other amphibians. It has even caused some kinds to die out completely. Infection by this fungus seems to be going up. This may be due to global warming.

SCIENTISTS ARE HARD AT WORK TRYING TO FIND OUT HOW TO FIGHT CHYTRID FUNGUS.

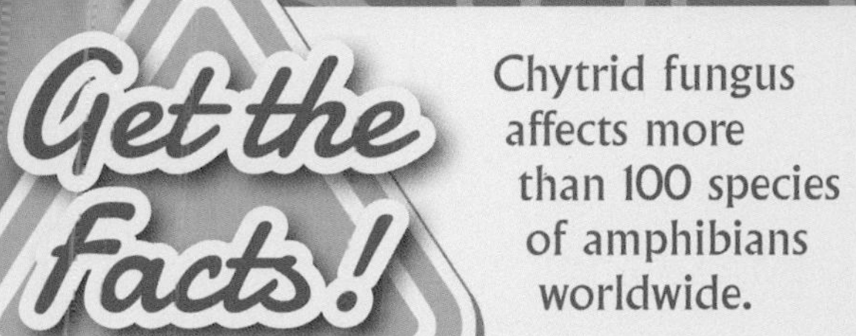

Several species of poison dart frogs are in danger. Some people are trying to preserve rain forests, or keep them in their natural state, to make sure no poison dart frogs go extinct, or totally die out.

DISAPPEARING HABITAT

Poison dart frogs eat **insects** and centipedes. Without these frogs, there would be too many insects and centipedes in the rain forest. In many areas of Central and South America, habitat loss is putting the frogs in danger. Rain forests are being destroyed by logging and mining.

GOLDEN POISON DART FROGS ARE AN ENDANGERED SPECIES. THIS MEANS THEY ARE IN DANGER OF DYING OUT COMPLETELY. LOSS OF HABITAT IS A MAJOR FACTOR IN THIS.

Clearing an area of land of all trees is called deforestation. This process harms all the animal populations that live there, not just poison dart frogs.

Poison dart frogs are in demand as pets. Many people want to keep them as pets for their beauty. This has brought down the numbers, or population, of some of the most brightly colored frogs in the wild. It has put their natural population in danger.

MEDICAL USES

Some effects of poisons can be good if they are controlled. For example, a person who is very ill might need a strong painkiller.

Poison dart frog toxins might be deadly, but scientists are finding ways to use them as **medicines**. Batrachotoxin was used to make a painkiller that is 200 times stronger than current painkillers. However, the dose needed to reduce pain is very close to the dose that would kill a person. It was not approved for use.

SCIENTISTS ARE ABLE TO MAKE BATRACHOTOXIN IN A LABORATORY. THIS WILL MAKE THE POISON EASIER TO STUDY, AND WILL KEEP POISON DART FROGS SAFE.

Scientists are learning about the human body by studying poison dart frogs and batrachotoxin.

GLOSSARY

absorb To take into the body through the skin.

cold-blooded Having a body temperature that's the same as the temperature of the surroundings.

fertilize To add male reproductive material to the female's eggs.

hatch To come out of an egg.

indigenous Having to do with the earliest known people living in an area.

inject To force a liquid into a living thing using a needle, stinger, or fangs.

insect A small, often winged, animal with six legs and three main body parts.

mate To come together to produce babies.

medcine Drug used to make a sick person well.

mimic To closely copy the looks or behaviors of another person or animal.

secrete To produce or discharge from a gland or a cell.

species A group of plants or animals that are all of the same kind.

FOR MORE INFORMATION

Grack, Rachel. *Poison Dart Frogs*. Minneapolis, MN: Bellwether Media, 2019.

Zalewski, Aubrey. *Poison Dart Frogs*. North Mankato, MN: Capstone Press, 2019.

Poison Dart Frog
animals.net/poison-dart-frog/
Read more about poison dart frogs and see photos of different species.

Poison Frog
kids.sandiegozoowildlifealliance.org/index.php/animals/poison-frog
Learn much more about poison dart frogs from this colorful and detailed site from the San Diego Zoo.

INDEX